MW00460463

I ONCE HAD A DATE NAMED **LUST**:

BREAKING FREE FROM SEX AND LOVE ADDICTION

By

DR. SIMON V. WHITTAKER

9/20/2015

Nicole & Melvin —

Be Free !
(Luke 22:31-32)

Simon

All rights reserved.

This book or no parts of this book may be reproduced, transmitted in any form or by any means electronic, mechanical, photocopy, recording or otherwise without written permission from the author.

First published in Greensboro, North Carolina

Copyright © 2010 by Dr. Simon Whittaker

ISBN: 978-0-9827287-2-7

Third Printing: 2011

DEDICATION

To my parents and my brother in memoriam - thanks.
To my sister-in-law, Kelly, and my nieces and nephews
(Kelly, Adam, Eddie, Ellen, Kathy), I am inspired by your
resilience.

To my incredible wife, Tyra, you are more than I deserve.
I pray that I grow to a point of being truly worthy of your
love. As the Bible says I have found a wife, a good thing,
so I am indeed blessed. To my daughter, Grace, you are an
incredible gift from God. You are my reminder of God's
amazing grace.

To those who feel trapped in a world of lust and
relationship addiction, this book is dedicated to you and the
future that God desires for you.

Acknowledgements

For their support in this endeavor, I would like to extend my heartfelt appreciation to:

My wife, Dr. Tyra Turner Whittaker, LPC, CRC, without your persistent encouragement this book would not exist. Your confidence in me empowers me to do those things that I should do.

Keith Shuert, Ed.D., thanks so much for your careful review and thoughtful feedback for the book.

Joe Bruyninckx, thanks so much for all of your encouragement and support. Thanks for your encouragement in completing this book.

Alicia Brown, MS, CRC, thanks for your thoughtful review and feedback regarding the book.

James P. Murray, thanks for your editing skills and encouragement to write the book, and for working within a tight timeline.

FOREWORD

Once in a lifetime, a book is written that reveals the greatness of the human spirit, and at the same time, challenges the very weakness of man. *I Once Had a Date Named Lust: Breaking Free from Sex and Love Addiction* provides the reader with a very candid look at the temptations experienced by men and women alike. It also bluntly exposes the irrational beliefs and actions taken by individuals impacted by sexual lust. Dr. Simon Whittaker's willingness to share his journey allows the reader to remove every defense mechanism in the form of lies, excuses, rationalizations, and triggers in an effort to be free from the bondage that comes from yielding to sexual temptation. The knowledge and tools given to the reader are very practical and effective. If you desire to grow in your relationship with Jesus Christ, to be emotionally and physically faithful to your spouse, to practice self-control, and to live victoriously without fearing that temptation will cost you your profession, family, and livelihood, then this book is for you!

Keith Shuert, Ed.D.

WARNING!

Reading past this point can quickly and drastically change your life! Many readers have experienced immediate peace, freedom, victory, and power over temptation at home, work, and other aspects of their lives. Most have reported a renewed appreciation and love for their significant others. Families are being rejoined and generational curses of yielding to lust and temptation have been broken.

I can do all things through Christ who strengthens me – Phil 4:13

(31) And the Lord said, Simon, Simon, behold, Satan hath desired to have you, that he may sift you as wheat: (32) But I have prayed for thee, that thy faith fail not: and when thou art converted, strengthen thy brethren. (Luke 22:31-32, King James Version)

This Book Answers the Following Questions:

1. Why do I need this book?

2. How would my life be better if I was able to build a life of sexual integrity?

3. Don't you want to be a better husband or wife? Here is how you can be.

4. Don't you want to be a better father or mother? Here is how you can be.

5. Can a recovery team (counselor, sponsor, recovery group, etc.) help you avoid key pitfalls?

6. How do I pursue my purpose, and experience a sense of fulfillment and achievement?

TABLE OF CONTENTS

Part I

An Original Recipe:

A Testimony in the Making

Chapter 1

My Story

The Terrible Threes—Terror at Home

Screaming, crashing noises, and terror. These were my earliest memories. I was three years old and I was horrified. My father had just come home in a drunken rage. My mother put me inside a large cabinet in an attempt to protect me from the violence. I believe my brother was in the cabinet with me, but I was so scared I do not remember for sure. It was dark in the cabinet. There were noises that sounded like the house was being destroyed. I heard yelling and screaming. After what seemed like an eternity . . . the noises stopped. My father had left the house.

My mother took me out of the cabinet. I looked around the house. Through my very young eyes, I saw that our house had been destroyed. The furniture was turned over and broken and there was blood on the floor. My mother's face was bruised; it was swollen and covered with blood because my father had beaten her badly. I remember looking in the bathroom. I saw her hair in the toilet. My father had torn the wig off her head.

My mother grabbed me and my brother. She said, "We have to leave right now before your father comes back." We left through the back door and ran as fast as we could.

I don't remember the name of the place where we stayed that night. It must have been a motel. We were in a room by ourselves (my mother, my brother and I) and no other people were around. My mother had a can of tuna for the three of us to share. The only other thing I remember about that particular night is the feeling that my father would not find us—for the rest of the night we would be safe. Unfortunately, that was the first of many times that we would have to leave home to find safety.

The next memory I have of my father also occurred when I was about three years old. I think it was a few months after the previous incident. He was on the porch on the other side of the front door, which was constructed of a wooden frame and glass near the top. The door was closed; my mother had locked my father out of the house. I remember hearing my father put his fist through the glass. He forced his way into the house and his hand was cut and bleeding badly. Once again, I was terrified.

When I was about five years old, I asked my mother, "Why is daddy always trying to hurt us?" She tried to explain that he got mean when he drank liquor. She tried to convince me that he still cared about us, but when he drank, it was as if he became a different person. So, I told Mom, if drinking makes him mean and makes him want to hurt us, then he needs to stop drinking. As a child, I didn't understand why he would not stop drinking with all of the pain that he was causing the people he said he cared about.

Chapter 2

The Perfect Recipe to Create an Addict

The Ingredients

One part physical abuse and one part emotional abuse: *The victim becomes the perpetrator.*

After many years of trying to figure out what was wrong with me and how I got this way, I was told by my sponsor to find out more about my father. I remember finding out from my mother that my father's father was a violent alcoholic. She also told me that was why my paternal grandparents divorced. Later on, after breaking my vow to never speak to anyone on my father's side of the family, I spoke to my father's older brother. He told me more about my paternal grandfather's drinking and that he dropped out of school before completing high school. I was amazed that my father was raised by an abusive, alcoholic father and became an abusive, alcoholic father himself. He ended up repeating the cycle of chaos.

It took many years for me to come to believe he did not want that to happen. For years, I thought he was trying to create chaos in our family. After reading scores of books about addiction and sick family patterns, seeing a counselor, and working through my own recovery programs, I finally learned my father's goal was not to make my mother, my brother and me miserable. I used to think that was his main goal in life. I learned that he was not a bad person. He was a sick person; he was a hurt person. And, as I've heard it said before, hurt people tend to hurt people. I did not know it at the time, but I was a recipe in process. My father, without realizing it, added the first ingredient-- physical abuse.

One part physical abuse added:

As long as I can remember, my father seemed to hate me. He constantly used phrases like: "Can't you do anything right?" and "You'll never amount to anything." If that doesn't sound familiar, congratulations—but please don't think you don't have any issues. If the negative statements do sound familiar, there's help for you within these pages.

In fact, here is the first and most important thing to remember about parents, and people in general, who are negative toward you. The issue is usually about them, not about you. Accepting that fact will give you a sense of freedom that money cannot buy. If you don't believe me, please continue to read and ask other credible professionals.

During one out of the hundreds of arguments my parents had before they finally divorced, my father yelled out: "I never wanted to have that <expletive><expletive> in the first place." (He was referring to me and describing that he never wanted to have me in the first place). Then I heard my mother say, "Don't say that, he (meaning me) might hear you." Then, my father made it clear that he did not care if I heard or not (using his very colorful, explicit language again). That statement was not as troubling to my young psyche as you might think. I was between 8 and 10 years old at the time. The reason that his statement didn't bother me as much as some might have thought is that he already treated me like he hated me, so I wasn't surprised to hear him say how he felt about me. As I stated earlier, if people have an issue with you, the issue is not about you, often it's about them.

I learned many years later that my mother had gotten pregnant with me while she and my father were dating. Then, at the age of 20, he found himself getting married to my mother who was already several months pregnant with me. So he felt trapped into marrying my mother and taking on the responsibility of being a father. He didn't bargain for all of that; he just wanted to have sex with my mother. So, my father went from being a relatively carefree, single man to being weighed down with a wife and child—what a bummer! No wonder he was upset. So, he took out his frustration on my mother, my brother and me. It seemed that every time he looked at me, he blamed me for his unhappiness. Hence, the name-calling: "You're stupid, you're dumb, you'll never amount to anything, and I don't know why I even had you." It was never about me. It was really about him. Hence, he added one part emotional abuse.

One part emotional abuse added:

It took a while to realize that he gave me the best that he had. He did the best that he could with the knowledge, understanding, and issues he had at the time. As one of my sponsors mentioned, if my father had addressed his demons, I would not have inherited them. But, the joy in this process is that I get to accept responsibility for my life.

As an adult, I'm responsible for what I do with my life now. The choices that I make will determine my destiny.

I was fortunate to have lived with both of my biological parents. My father was a plumber. My mother was a social worker. She had great advice for other families, while our family was falling apart. But, there was something about my mother that I didn't know. For years, I did not want to admit that she had a drinking problem. She was a closet drinker, usually drinking in her bedroom with the door closed. She didn't get violent like my father. So, it was not easy to see how much she drank; it was easy to ignore the impact of her drinking.

My mom was sweet, kind and loving. She made it clear through her actions that she loved me, my brother, and even my father. She worked at a full-time job for the state of Michigan. She cooked our meals, mostly on the weekend, and we usually ate those meals during the week. She assigned my brother and I to help keep the house clean. When we went clothes shopping, my mother usually did not buy clothes for herself. She had very little money and she would say that she would buy clothes for herself after she got clothes for us. She made many sacrifices for us.

But, when my father had a crisis, everything stopped in our household and my mother was not emotionally available for my brother and me. She would say things like, "I need to go and help your father." Or, "We need to go and help your father."

Those are the things that she would say when his drinking led to him being arrested or when his drinking led to him getting into fights or being physically hurt. Or, there were times that he just wouldn't come home and my mother would spend the night worrying about him. From my child and adolescent perspective, the end result was the same. My mother may have been physically at home, but she was not accessible to my brother and me. Physically, she may have been present, but emotionally she wasn't there. Because of my father's drinking and drug problems, it seemed that there was always a crisis that demanded my mother's attention.

One part physical abandonment added and One part emotional abandonment added:

As with any recipe, the ingredients have to be mixed together and stirred thoroughly. When the ingredients are mixed together, they work together and have a greater impact than they would have individually. In addition to mixing the ingredients together, the mixture is also heated. The heat creates stress. As in most cases, when the system is under stress, all of the weaknesses become amplified and easily visible.

The good is really good, but the bad can be dangerous and destroy you--and your family. So, for several decades, I've been under the stress of life . . . trying to live life with all of my weaknesses and character defects. Eventually my character defects led to so much pain that I was forced to deal with them.

Even in the dysfunction of my childhood home, there was the sense that God and the church were important. I don't ever recall going to church as a family, but there were times that my father would drive my brother and I to his mother's church. I don't remember much about Big Mama's church except singing in the choir for a while. A few years later as a pre-teen and a young teenager my brother and I would walk to a nearby church instead of getting a ride to Big Mama's church. So, from an early age I was familiar with reading my Bible and praying.

Years later, as my relationship with my second fiancée began to unravel, I found myself doing a whole lot of Bible-reading and praying. But I needed additional help.

So, what are these issues and character defects of mine? Here's the short list: low self-esteem, fear of abandonment, fear of intimacy, love addiction, lust, porn, and obsession with sex.

What happened to get me on the road to recovery? The second woman I was engaged to was trying to convince me that I had issues. She wanted to leave me. My love addict was terrified of abandonment, and she was flirting with other men.

The pain of that relationship drove me to get additional help. Yes, even with my big male ego, I went to get help--a counselor and recovery program. The counselor helped me to better understand my issues and the dynamics of my relationship. The recovery program and especially my sponsor helped me to get through the pain of abandonment, and work through my issues.

Chapter 3

Sponsorship

I use the terms sponsor, recovery mentor, and mentor somewhat synonymously. What exactly is a sponsor? A sponsor is just someone who has been successful in overcoming a specific type of challenge. A recovering alcoholic who has been able to stay sober for a year or more and is able to now guide someone through the process of getting and staying sober can be a sponsor. Someone who has recovered from co-dependence or love addiction and is able to guide someone else through the process is a sponsor. A recovering drug addict who has been able to stay clean for a year or more and is able to guide someone else through the processes of getting clean and living free from the use of drugs is a sponsor.

Sponsors come in all kinds of varieties: they can help people with issues like obsessive overwork, obsessive-compulsive relationships, overeating, sex and lust, spending, gambling, entertainment (yes, many people are addicted to television and video games). Of course this is the short list. People can go overboard about doing too much of just about anything.

I once heard someone say that the purpose of an addiction is to medicate intolerable reality. So, if people are using substances, such as drugs and alcohol, and behaviors to avoid dealing with reality, a sponsor can help people live their lives without having to escape by using substances and behaviors.

Of course, sponsors are just one resource that a person might use. There are other resources such as medical doctors, counselors, etc. A sponsor is just a mentor who has overcome a specific challenge and is able and willing to guide someone else through the process.

Why Do You Need a Sponsor?

Keep in mind that a sponsor has overcome a specific challenge and is able and willing to help you overcome that challenge. There are several people who may be able to assist you in overcoming a specific challenge. If you're trying to overcome challenges that are keeping you from being all that God created you to be, then you owe it to God, yourself, and your loved ones to use whatever reasonable means you can to overcome those challenges. If you need a medical doctor or counselor, then find someone who can assist you.

It's also important that you never neglect the guidance of the Holy Spirit. The Holy Spirit can give you insight into the deeper issues that are blocking you. So, in addition to the Holy Spirit and studying God's Word, you may also want to find a knowledgeable professional who can assist you in overcoming your challenges.

I have used several professionals to assist me in overcoming numerous challenges: including medical doctors, counselors, recovery groups, and sponsors. I have received great benefit from them. However, the greatest benefit by far has come in the form of my sponsors -- godly men who have helped me to live life on life's terms, and not medicate my pain with negative substances and behaviors.

Now, back to the original question, why do you need a sponsor? It's because everyone has strengths, weaknesses, and issues. If you have major issues that are stopping you from being all that God has called you to be you may be in one of three categories:

Category 1: it's a small social issue: things in this category involve over eating, drinking, procrastination, and other "bad habits" or things that are negative, but things that you can stop easily if you make up your mind to do so or if there is enough social pressure.

Category 2: this issue has a negative impact and some control over you. You have trouble saying no to this temptation. For example, with over eating, maybe you've tried to curb your appetite but you can't. With drinking or smoking, you've been told by a doctor that you have to stop or you'll die an early death or have severe health problems, but you've tried and prayed and you just can't stop. You may have even gone to see a counselor, but you still can't stop.

Category 3: this is an issue that has taken control of your life. You've done all that you know how to do, but it still has control of you. You have prayed, you've studied God's Word, you have tried to cut back, and you have seen a counselor or physician.

Here is a different way to look at these categories, using alcohol as an example. Let's take Jonathan for example. He's a young professional, college-educated and appears to have it all together. A few years ago, he began going out with his friends more frequently to the local bar. At first, he really went just because he enjoyed the company (category 1). They all get along so well together.

Five years ago, some of his friends began to tell him that maybe he was drinking too much. But, he blew them off, saying that they just didn't know how to loosen up enough. Five years ago, he was confident that if he really wanted to stop he could have. After all he had only been drinking for a couple of weeks; he had been to the bar two Fridays in a row with coworkers. By his third year of drinking, he was planning his work schedule and weekend activities around his drinking. He would try to get to work early so that he could leave work to get to the bar before it got crowded (that's one of the joys of having a flexible work schedule).

He used to spend time with his wife on Friday nights; it used to be their date night. But, since she won't join him at the bar on Friday evenings, he said they had to forgo their date night because he has to go to the bar to unwind after a long, hard week at the office. He's becoming more irritable and unreliable. His marriage is falling apart. Jonathan and his wife have emotional distance between them, but he doesn't even notice it. She's asked for more of his time, but that would cut into his drinking time—he couldn't let that happen. (Category 2).

Now, five years later, he and his wife don't spend much time together at all. They still live in the same house, for now. But they don't have much to talk about. He doesn't initiate conversations because he's afraid she will bring up his drinking and how it's destroying their marriage. She doesn't talk much because it's hard to have a conversation by yourself or with a husband who is irritable and full of anger. Since his friends at the bar seem to understand him, he spends more time with them. He now has new friends.

Then, one afternoon, he sees his doctor, who tells him that his drinking is really taking a toll on his health and that he needs to drink in moderation or stop drinking all together. He becomes resentful at the doctor for suggesting that he might have a drinking problem, so he does the next logical thing that any addict would do. He goes to the bar to get drunk. After leaving the bar, while driving home, he gets into an accident, smashing his car into a tree. When the police and ambulance arrive, he's charged with driving under the influence and is taken to the hospital for his injuries. His license is now suspended.

A few days later, after he's released from the hospital, he does the next logical thing that any addict would do . . . he goes to his favorite bar to spend time with his friends (translation to get drunk), and he tries to figure out a way that he can drink and drive without the police giving him a hard time. (Category 3).

Of course, looking in from the outside, it's easy to see Jonathan's insanity. But Jonathan lives his life in that craziness so he can't see it. Of course, if you used to live in that kind of insanity, have been sober for several years, and have helped others get out of it, you can see the insanity. In fact, you may even be able to predict what will happen next in the cycle.

If you're immersed in your own insanity, you probably can't see it clearly either. That's one of the issues people often have. So, why do you need a sponsor? Because depending on the issue you have, you may not even live long enough to figure out what to do to get yourself out of it.

If you're addicted to pornography, how many years, how many decades, and how many relationships will you destroy before you begin to get a handle on the issue? If you are addicted to sex or relationships, how many marriages do you have to destroy before you start to do something about it? If you're on the verge of destroying your first marriage because of a sex, porn, or relationship addiction, do you think that if your next wife is just the right woman that will solve your problems? Are you thinking, I won't have to put up with all of that nagging with the next woman I date. My wife is forever nagging me and getting on my case. She drove me to the other woman. If she wouldn't act like my mother, trying to boss me around, I wouldn't mind spending more time with her. Many men think. . . . If my wife would just give me more sex, I wouldn't have this issue. She just needs to understand that my having an affair is good for our marriage. It keeps me from putting so much pressure on her for sex and when I'm not pressuring her for sex, we get along so much better.

Some men will spend a lifetime trying to figure out what's wrong with their relationship with their wife, fiancée, or girlfriend. (Of course, if you're married or engaged and you're involved in another "romantic" relationship, you should expect chaos and problems.)

- If you're married and you're having sex with anyone other than your spouse, you need a sponsor. If you're engaged and you're already cheating on her, then you need a sponsor. If you happen to be unmarried and your values regarding sex state that you should not be having sex before marriage, then you need a sponsor. If you view pornography and feel guilty about it, then you need a sponsor.

- Of course, if you don't feel any guilt, you probably aren't ready to address the issue. If you've tried to stop viewing pornography and keep going back to it, then you need a sponsor. If your wife, fiancée, or girlfriend has gotten into an argument with you about your pornography, you need a sponsor. If your wife has threatened to leave because of your affairs or your pornography addiction, then you need a sponsor.

- If you've started an emotional affair and have tried to end it but can't, you need a sponsor. So, what is an emotional affair? How do you know if you're in an emotional affair? If you're wondering if you're in an emotional affair, then you probably are.

- But, just in case you're still wondering, here are a few signs:

(1) You look forward to seeing the person more than your wife or fiancée.

(2) You go out of your way to make flattering comments to that person (that you wouldn't say to others). For example, you might mention to Julie, a co-worker, "Your hair looks great today. Is she the

only woman you saw with great looking hair today? Of course not. So, why did she get that compliment and not the other women with great looking hair? (3) You make special note of things that she likes, things that she lacks, or things that are important to her and then you go out of your way to meet that need? In other words, you do things to endear yourself to her, to get her to feel that you are her savior. Here is an example: you notice that she drinks coffee with two sugars (but she only uses artificial sweetener) and one cream, and she likes to have it stirred with a spoon, not a straw or a stirrer. So, you stopped by the break room to get it for her, and you fix it just the way she likes it--including the spoon. How does your wife take her coffee?

Here is an example of something she lacks: Julie comes to work and she is clearly depressed about something. She might mention that she and her longtime boyfriend have broken up. She's in a lot of pain. You ask her what's wrong and she tells you about the breakup and the pain that she's in. You listen to her very, very attentively. You notice that she feels that her ex-boyfriend took her for granted and did not appreciate her. You think you sense a need, and you do, but it's a distorted need.

What you think you detect is a need for her to feel special and wanted. So, you proceed to tell her how awful her ex-boyfriend is and if you were him you would treat her like a queen. You begin to spout a lot of other sick relationship "pick-up" lines. You convince yourself that what she needs is to feel desirable as a woman. You convince yourself that you are meeting her need and doing something important for her. But, in essence you are doing something for you. You're only telling her those things so that she will see you in a greater light, think better of you, and be drawn toward you. Of course you try to convince yourself that all you did was help a coworker. But, when you get home you don't bother to tell your wife what you told Julie, about how you would treat her like a queen if you were her man.

Of course, two months ago, when Julie was in pain and wanted to talk about her sick grandmother, you weren't nearly as attentive. Last month, she was trying to tell you about how she and her boyfriend were going to help grandma with her medical treatment. You didn't seem to have time then, but now you're attentive. Now you care. You're such a humanitarian. How can Julie hope to survive without you? You told your wife, "Oh, Julie's grandma is having some problems and Julie and her boyfriend are trying to help out." But, this time you didn't mention that

Julie broke up with her boyfriend and you provided a much-needed shoulder for her to cry on. If she needs a shoulder to cry on, ask her to contact one of her female friends. Beyond listening to her (in a limited way) and praying for her, there is very little help you can offer. But, if you try to do more, you can cause great harm. Of course by now, you're thinking why can't I just compliment Julie and tell her how wonderful she is and how well I would treat her? You know the answer to that, but since you want to play dumb, here's the answer. You're not healthy enough to do that. What will happen is that you'll tell her how wonderful she is, how well you'd treat her, and all of the things that you would do for her. Because of her pain, she's in a very vulnerable state, and more susceptible to your lies. Because of her pain, she wants to believe what you're telling her.

Over the ensuing weeks and months, you continue to shower her with sweet words and compliments and you help to build up her self-esteem, which was crushed by the knucklehead she used to date. Within a few short months, she is responding with compliments toward you telling you how wonderful you are and giving you the kind of attention you've always wanted. For the first time in years, you actually look forward to going to work. Of course, when your wife notices that you're excited about going to work, you lie to her and tell her something about feeling really good about some work project.

You know that you need to stop this insanity and end the emotional affair. But, you don't. Of course by now, you've started to pay more attention to the clothes that you wear to work. You start wearing cologne to work; you never did that before. You even start getting to work a few minutes early. (That's really unusual for you.) You've been fantasizing about Julie and all the wild passion that the two of you will share. Of course, you feel some guilt about the fact that you're married. But, it's been many, many months now since your conscience first told you that you needed to end the emotional affair. You can't end it now. It's too exciting. You're in too deep. You're too committed.

So, you and Julie set up a time for your rendezvous. The timing is perfect. You have to go out of town on "business" and she can come with you. You have sex with Julie in the hotel over the course of several days. As you head home, the guilt hits you. The reality sets in. You've committed adultery. You feel horrible. The affair continues because you don't have the guts to tell your wife what you've done, and you don't have the guts to end the affair. You'd like to think that you're a super stud and Julie and your wife can't live without you. The truth is far from flattering. It's not that you're a bad person. The truth is that emotionally and spiritually, you're a sick person and a coward.

So, how does it end? You know how it ends. Your ego leads you to believe that you can continue to live a double life. You think you can pretend to be a fully devoted and loving husband and father while also having an affair. I know you think you can be a loving father while cheating on your wife, the mother of your children. But, things are different now . . . you have two women, which means that you have choices. When your wife is giving you a hard time, making demands, and nagging you, you can go see your mistress, and complain to her about how badly your wife treats you and how you deserve better. (That sounds familiar doesn't it? That's the same thing you did when her knucklehead boyfriend left her. Only this time, you're the knucklehead.)

Your relationship with Julie, your mistress, doesn't have much depth, and she doesn't demand a lot--yet. She's just excited about having your company, and she's excited about how well you treat her. Julie thinks the relationship with you is wonderful. In fact it's, beyond wonderful. The relationship is all that she dreamed of, except for the fact that you're a liar and you can't be trusted. You're thinking, who me, a liar? I'm a great guy. I know, I know. Great guys can be liars, too. Of course, you're a liar. When you married your wife, you made a vow to be true to her. Do you remember that part of the wedding ceremony about forsaking all others, being true to her? You're a liar because you made a vow and you have broken it and continue to do so every week when you meet with Julie for sex. Obviously, you can't be trusted. If you'll cheat on your wife, who you vowed to be true to and who you had children with, how can she trust you? And if your wife can't trust you, why should anyone else?

Two of the reasons that you felt so much more passion with Julie than with your wife are because (1) affairs are sprints; (2) affairs involve fantasy and a distortion of reality. In a very elementary sense, there is a great distinction between running 100 yards and running 26.2 miles.

Affairs are like Sprints. If you're an average person who can jog around your block (even if the pace is so slow, it almost looks like a fast walk), you could run 100 yards. You could pretend to be a track star and probably convince some people that you are. But, very few people can run a marathon unless they undergo some very intense specific training. If you run a marathon (26.2) miles without preparation, first of all you probably won't be able to complete it. If you do, you're going to be hurting in places that you didn't know existed, and every physical weakness you have will become apparent. If you haven't conditioned your thighs, it will show. If your knees are weak the stress from the marathon will show. If the muscles in your back are weak, it will show. Because a marathon is so demanding, your weaknesses will show and they will be amplified. The small knee pain that you had before the marathon started will be amplified before you hit the 12 mile mark.

Affairs are like 100-yard sprints. You can put your best foot forward to tell the right lies and create the persona of a classy guy. You can get away with that in an affair because it's a sprint. You meet her once a week. You have a meal and you have sex and pretend to be someone you're not (cool, confident). When you're having an affair, she sees you at your best physically (not morally, of course). You say the right things, you appear to be kind and patient with her; you appear to be a gentleman. But, because it's an affair, it's a sprint, you can pull it off. You only have to do that once or twice a week for a few hours.

Marriages are like Marathons. But marriage is different: it's a marathon. Marriage is for grownups. Since marriage is a marathon, your wife gets to see things that your mistress doesn't. You wife gets to see your anger when things aren't going well. She gets to see how you react under pressure. You're issues become apparent in the marriage. If you are unkind, it becomes evident. If you have a short temper, it becomes evident. If you're messy and don't clean up after yourself, it become evident. All the weaknesses and issues you hide during the sprint become apparent and visible during the marathon. If your mistress knew how you perform during the marathon, what you're really like, she might think twice about wanting a more permanent relationship with you.

You enjoy every rendezvous with Julie. Those times are hot and passionate. She doesn't complain, she doesn't put demands on you, she doesn't nag you. It's great. Your wife on the other hand . . . yes, she does complain. She always has things for you to fix. Fix this, fix that, she wants to remodel the kitchen; she wants new furniture for the bedroom and the living room. She wants more family time with you and the kids. When the two of you do have sex, it's at the end of a very long day, after the kids get to bed, and it doesn't seem nearly as passionate as sex with Julie. You begin to think if only I weren't burdened down with my wife. Julie, the kids, and I could have a great life together.

Chapter 4

Affairs Involve Fantasy and a Distortion of Reality

The Fantasy of the Affair

Affairs involve fantasy, and they distort reality. Robert and Susan, another couple involved a long-standing affair, couldn't see that they were living in a distorted reality. Their relationship seemed wonderful and passionate. But, those who are involved in affairs often don't recognize their own insanity.

Robert and Susan both had fantasies. Susan's fantasy was that Robert made her feel beautiful, desirable, worthy to be treated like a queen. The fantasy was that if she had more of Robert's love, adoration and admiration, she would be special. So she felt that she had to have that relationship. What she didn't realize is that Robert doesn't have that much power; no one does. Susan was already special because she was created in God's image. But, somewhere along the way, she forgot that.

Robert's fantasy was that if he was with Susan, he would feel sexy, desirable, and powerful. She cares about his opinion. She's really excited to see him . . . and the sex is passionate. There are several reasons that sex with Susan seems more passionate.

Instead of passion, a better phrase would be exciting-misery. It's exciting because it's something they shouldn't be doing. Somewhat similar to the excitement that some get from looking at pornography, stealing office supplies from work, shoplifting a valuable item from the store, or pushing the accelerator of your car all the way to the floor on an open stretch of highway to see how fast the car can go. Now that's exciting. But, there's also a component of misery because there are consequences for getting caught. Looking at pornography could cost you an important relationship. Stealing office supplies could get you fired. Shoplifting could win you an all-expenses-paid trip to your local jail. Driving over 100 miles per hour on the freeway could provide you with the opportunity to trade in your driver's license for a city bus pass—hooray! How do you like that travel upgrade?

Robert's fantasy involved exciting misery: the excitement of having forbidden sex with his mistress and the misery of knowing that if he's caught, his life could unravel. Since Susan was younger than Robert, and she always told him how good he looked, he felt sexy, he felt powerful, he felt desirable, he felt like a stud. His ego loved it.

Then, because Robert has been with Susan for a long while and he treats her so well, she wants more of his time. That's not what he wanted. She begins making demands, wanting him to prove his love for her. B*uy me this; buy me that; leave your wife; marry me.* You know the drill. Now he begins to feel that both his wife and his mistress are causing all kinds of problems. So, when Susan gets on his nerves, he spends more time at home with his wife. When his wife gets on his nerves, he spends more time with Susan. He begins to feel like a victim, and yet, he's responsible for all the chaos.

Then it happens. One day, his wife finds undeniable proof of his ongoing affair with Susan. He's terrified. He had fantasized about being able to have a life with Susan, but then he continues with a series of stupid actions.

Stupid Things (some) Men Do in Relationships
(Note: more women are beginning to do these stupid things too.)

STMD #1 (Stupid things men do in Relationships) - Keeping secrets. If you can't tell your wife, it's probably something you shouldn't be doing. (See the Robert and Susan example above.)

STMD #2 (Stupid things men do in Relationships): fantasizing that having an affair will solve your relationship problems.

STMD #3 (Stupid things men do in Relationships) - Lying (see example of Robert lying to Susan about how horrible his wife is).

STMD #4 (Stupid things men do in Relationships) - Confusing reality and fantasy (see example of the affair with Susan)

A friend of mine once said it like this, referring to alcoholism: if a man is at a bar and he drank half of his cocktail and then notices that there is a fly in it. He says, "What's that fly doing in my drink?" pushes the drink away and engages in a conversation with the man next to him. (The man in this situation is a social drinker –

category 1. He may enjoy drinking with others, but the thought of having a fly in his drink is repulsive).

On the other hand, if the man at the bar is a category 2 drinker, and notices that there is a fly in his drink, he'll use his fingers to get the fly out of his drink and then he'll finish the rest of his drink. (He's more concerned about finishing his drink than he is about germs from the fly).

But, if the man is a category 3 drinker, a full-blown alcoholic, his response to the fly tells the whole story. He sees the fly. He will pick the fly out of his drink. He drinks his drink. Then he opens his mouth, holds the fly over his open mouth, and squeezes the fly to get any liquor that the fly may have absorbed.

If you have issues that are stopping you from being all that God has called you to be, you won't live long enough to figure them out on your own. If you have severe issues with alcohol, it's very likely that you won't live long enough to figure out how to live free of it.

The goal is to help you deal with life on life's terms, not to medicate and hide from life's challenges through the use of drugs, alcohol, food, sex, gambling, television, video games, etc. (Do you get the idea or do I need to continue with the list?) If you're thinking to yourself, "I don't have any of those issues," let me know, and I'll include your issues in the next edition of this book. The truth is: all of us have issues, but some issues may be more severe than others.

Getting Help

So, what can you do if you really want to get help? There are several options. A good counselor can be a god-send, and help to provide insight regarding the basis for one or more of your issues. You can contact a counselor who is a member of a mental health organization or one who has a private practice. You should be prepared to pay when seeing a counselor since most charge a fee for their services. In addition, some members of the clergy are very skilled and experienced in providing lay counseling. (See the Love Addict Assessment, Appendix B. Also, see the Sex Addiction Assessment, Appendix C. These will provide additional information about love and sex addiction.)

Recovery groups are another option used by many people. Typically, there are no fees required and people are helped by those in the group who have been successful in overcoming the issue that you may be struggling with.

Another option is to work with a mentor, sometimes called a sponsor, who has been successful in overcoming the issue that's troubling you. This is a person who is available to assist you by guiding you through the challenges that are common in overcoming the specific issue that you face. In working with a sponsor, you will also learn how to become a sponsor and help others.

Some people may use a combination of these resources (counseling, recovery groups, sponsor) to overcome their specific challenge.

How would your life be better if you used a sponsor?

The purpose of a sponsor is to help you overcome a specific challenge. For our purposes, the sponsor would help you overcome your addiction, or unhealthy behaviors, regarding sex, lust, love or porn. If you're reading this book, you may have a problem with one or a combination of these challenges.

What are the characteristics of a good sponsor?

What are the characteristics of a good sponsor?

• They have joy, or at least serenity, regarding their
own recovery.

• They have a comfortable time of recovery themselves
(someone with at least a year of sexual
integrity/sexual purity).

• They are further along than you in recovery.

• They do recovery work, to maintain their own
recovery, on a regular basis (ideally daily).

• They are trustworthy and able to maintain strict
confidentiality.

• They have a genuine relationship with God.

• They maintain and enhance their relationship with
God on a regular (ideally on a daily basis).

• They view their recovery as the top priority in their
lives. If you're addicted to porn, sex, lust, or are a
love addict, that's your god. Working your

recovery program means putting your recovery first, which means putting your current god aside so that God can be first

A good sponsor can help in several ways. A good sponsor:

- Can provide hope that you can find recovery from your addiction (when you're in the midst of the pain of your addiction, there is nothing like being able to see people who are free of the hold that addiction had on them).
- Can provide a safe person who understands and practices confidentiality.
- Can provide hope from the perspective of someone who has been through similar circumstances.
- Can provide specific, practical tools to help you.
- Can provide insight about specific pitfalls and triggers that may lead you to acting out.

- Can provide an example of how to live a life of recovery in the real world.

There may also be some things that you get from a sponsor that you may not necessarily like, such as:

- Someone who is rougher on you than you'd like.

- Someone who doesn't tolerate excuses.

- Someone who helps you practice in the art of patience (when you don't like his suggestions).

Again, a sponsor is someone who can guide you in the process of overcoming a specific challenge. Working with a sponsor will provide opportunities and challenges, just like you would have in any relationship. One of the primary differences in this case is that your recovery, and the relationship with your sponsor, can have a significant impact on every other aspect of your life.

Don't you want to be a better husband? Here is how you can be.

The whole process of sponsorship is much more than getting help in overcoming a specific issue. Yes, the pain of your addictive and compulsive behavior may have brought you into recovery and led you to develop a relationship with a sponsor, but your willingness to change your life will determine the benefit you gain. If you're looking at pornography and cheating on your wife, the threat of her divorcing you and people knowing about your affairs may have forced you to seek help, but that won't keep you in recovery.

In general, addicts are people who are or have been in a lot of pain. Also, even in recovery we tend to be hard-headed people. If you're addicted to lust, pornography, sex, or if you're a love addict, you are probably already aware that there are some negative consequences and shame about what you do. If not, why don't you tell your co-workers about how often you masturbate while looking at pornography? Why don't you brag about the affairs that you have or the prostitutes that you've seen? Shame is one of the characteristics of those who are addicted.

So, if you happened to be a married man, and if you happened to be addicted to lust, pornography, or sex, are you the best husband you can be? Of course not! God has called husbands to be faithful to their wives. In addition, we are not supposed to look upon a woman to lust after her. That's not limited to real women in the flesh.

It also includes images of women in magazines, in videos, and online. These days, lust even comes in the form of text messages. There have been several politicians who have been forced to resign from their offices and in some cases even sentenced to jail time because of their affairs and text messages between them and the women they have cheated with. If you think you can be a good husband while being addicted to lust, pornography, and sex, you're kidding yourself. Until you get into recovery and actually have some sobriety, and stop acting out, you aren't even present in the relationship with your wife. Yes, you may have some brief instances of being present with her, but most of the time you just aren't there mentally and emotionally. While you're with her, you're thinking about how you can get your fix and how you can get her out of your hair so she won't get in the way. You're thinking about how you can look at your pornography without her finding out. You're wondering what lie you can tell, so that you can get some time away from her, get to the computer and log into one of the chat rooms so you can have virtual sex with one of the women there.

So, do you want to be a better husband? Yes, that's a real question. If you don't, I suggest that you skip this section for now. Don't waste your time and build any expectations about being a better husband if you're not willing to do what it takes. Recovery is tough. Recovery is for the courageous; it's not for cowards.

*Skip this section if you're **not** willing to do what it takes to be a better husband.*

****

Step 1: Get on your knees and acknowledge to God that your life is a mess. Get gut-level honest. Tell him about all of the things that you have done that are not in accordance with his will for you. That's right: all the lust, the pornography, the teasing and flirting, any marriages that you may have destroyed (including your own), any people that you have harmed, the women you have objectified, the women in the chat rooms that you have led on, and the things that you have thought about doing, but didn't have the guts to carry out. I know it sounds like a lot, but that's the cost of freedom. If you want to be free of your addiction, it will cost you--freedom ain't free! Then ask for his forgiveness.

Step 2: If you have an addiction, get help. This one is a little harder because men have egos--huge egos. It seems that the more messed up we are, the bigger our egos are. Many men will have difficulty admitting that they have a problem and even more trouble admitting that they are an addict. So, how do you know if you are a sex or love addict? (See Appendix B for the Love Addiction Assessment and Appendix C for the Sex Addiction Assessment.) Actually, the answer to the question is not as important as you might think. If you can't stop, then you're an addict. You've already shared with God all of the things that you did that were not in accordance with his will (in Step 1 or at some previous time). So, just stop. That's right: never look at pornography again (not another pornographic website, video, or magazine), never flirt with a woman you aren't married to (no more flirtatious talk, no more chat rooms, no more sexting), never have sex with anyone other than your wife.

If these behaviors are not obsessive, compulsive, addictive, you'll be able to stop. You don't need to get any additional help. You won't even have to ask God to take these desires away because they are within your control. If you're still reading, then, yes, you're an addict. Get help. You need someone you can talk to who can assist you. You may want to talk to a therapist or counselor, an interventionist, a relationship specialist, a sex specialist, a recovery program, a sponsor, or a qualified member of the clergy. You need to find someone you can talk to about these issues, and it needs to be someone who is unbiased and is both skilled and knowledgeable enough to be able to assist you. You will need to tell them about your past (that's right, telling it to God is good, but not sufficient). They will be able to tell you how much they need to know and the limitations (for example, if therapists or counselors learn that you have committed certain types of criminal activity, they are required to report it).

Step 3

Get help. You may want to contact a counselor or therapist. You may choose to seek help from a lay counselor affiliated with your religion or a civic organization. You may choose to get help from a support group. You might identify a sponsor to assist you. Many people in recovery benefit from a combination of the resources. These individuals will be an important part of your recovery.

Step 4

This step involves working with the helpers and resources that you identified in Step 3 to put together a plan for overcoming your addiction. Carry out the plan for your recovery. Every day there will be things you will need to do, or avoid, in order to stay on the path of recovery. You'll need to have one or more people that you are accountable to. For some this person may be an accountability partner, a mentor, or a sponsor. This person will help you follow your plan for staying in recovery from your addiction while also trying to live in the real world as you go to work, school, and interact with other people who are important to you.

If you're serious about being a better husband, that's what you need to do. If you've lied to yourself and tried to convince yourself that making more money will make you a better husband, you were wrong. If you told yourself that if you helped out more around the house and that would make you a better husband, you're wrong. If you told yourself that if you buy your wife more presents and gifts that would make you a better husband, you're wrong. None of those things matter while you are cheating on her. If you are lusting after women through pornography, videos, chat rooms, and websites, then emotionally you're cheating on her. If you're flirting, either virtually through text messages (sexting), chat rooms on the internet, or in person then you're having or trying to start an emotional affair and you're cheating on her (all you lack is the opportunity to connect in person). If you are having an affair, you're cheating on her. The bottom line is this, as long as you are cheating on her, none of those other things matter much (making more money, helping out around the house, getting gifts).

So, to be a better husband, first, you need to deal with the issues that keep you from being fully present in your relationship. Secondly, you need to deal with the issues that keep you from having the ability to be intimate in that relationship. Getting recovery from your lust addiction, pornography addiction, sex addiction, and love addiction will allow you to be fully present and give you the capability to be emotionally intimate with yourself and with your wife. Another bonus is the fact that you won't have to try to remember the string of lies that you've told in the past so you wouldn't get caught. And when your wife goes to use the computer, you won't have to worry about her finding the pornography you've downloaded or the porn websites that you've been to because you're now sexually pure, sexually sober, and you haven't been to any of those websites since you started recovery.

****

*Continue here for those who were **not** willing to do what it takes to be a better husband*

Don't you want to be a better father? Here is how you can be.

As a father, you might say, I still spend time with my children and I still provide for them. If you have children and you're addicted to lust, pornography, sex, or are a love addict (typically love addicts are women, but many men are love addicts, too) you aren't the best father that you could be to your children. Ouch! I know it hurts, but we have to deal with this. God has called fathers to train their children and part of that training is being a good example. The Bible says it this way: *"Train up a child in the way he should go: and when he is old, he will not depart from it."* (Proverbs 22:6, King James Version)

So, how does this impact your children? It affects your children in several ways. If you are addicted to lust, through lusting after women or lusting after images of women, you are hindering your ability to be the best father you can be. If you're addicted to pornography, pictures of women in magazines, in videos, or online, you can't be fully present when you're with your children. You may be with them physically, but when women walk by, your head is constantly turning as you engage in acts of lust. You access the computer to look at porn while the children are at school, and then you hope that they don't find those websites you've been secretly visiting. Since they're probably more tech savvy than you, you're constantly wondering if they'll find your electronic porn stash.

If you think you can be a great father while being addicted to lust, pornography, and sex, you're kidding yourself. Until you get into recovery, practice sobriety/integrity and stop acting out, you aren't even present in the relationship with your children. Also, because your children are dependent on you, they can't put the kind of pressure on you that your wife can.

For example, if you're cheating on your wife, she may divorce you, tell others that you've been having an affair, and sue you for alimony, custody of the children and child support. But, your children don't have that kind of power. They can't say, "Dad, I found the websites that you've been going to, and I know that you've been having an affair and seeing a prostitute. Even though I'm only 15, I'm going to divorce myself from you. I'm going to move out and start paying my own bills. How do you like that?"

The real pain that you'll feel as a father will come much later, after your children have moved out and are living on their own, and you realize that they don't want to have anything to do with you. Of course, you'll think, how could they do that? How could they ignore me and not want to spend time with me? If you haven't been present for them, during those tender moments when they needed you most, if you haven't helped them consistently along the way, they don't see you as their dad--you're just a sperm donor. I know you didn't want to hear that, but it's better to hear it from me now than from your children 10 years from now when you're wondering why your son or daughter didn't invite you to the wedding or tell you that you're now a grandfather.

The other issue is that your children will have trouble doing what you tell them to do, because if you're an addict and not addressing your addiction and getting better, they will see you as a person who doesn't have any integrity. If you're telling them they shouldn't smoke, shouldn't drink, and shouldn't engage in sex until marriage, and they know that you've been having affairs and are addicted to pornography, you won't have any credibility. As a parent, if you don't have integrity, then you don't have credibility. If you don't have integrity and credibility, then you don't have any real authority. If you don't have real authority the only way you'll be able to get your children to the things they don't want to do, such as homework or cleaning up around the house, is by threatening them or bullying them.

Sometimes there is a tendency to forget the important role that fathers play. You set the example for your sons and your daughters. You're teaching your sons what a man is supposed to be, how a man behaves, how a man treats his children. If you're married, you're also teaching them how a man treats his wife. You're teaching your daughters how a man behaves, how he should treat his daughters (it's the way you treat her). Also, if you're married you're teaching her how a husband should treat his wife. If you show me a woman who had a horrible relationship with her father, I'll show you a woman in a bad relationship today. You should expect your daughter to pick a man like her father, because in most cases she will. How would you feel if your daughter brought someone like you home and announced that she was going to marry him? Is that good news? If so, great. If not, that's just one more incentive to get sober. Often people have several motives for getting into recovery, like trying to save their romantic relationship or their marriage, their relationship with their children, or their job. But ultimately, you have to want to stay sober and live with sexual integrity for yourself.

So, do you want to be a better father? If you don't, I suggest that you skip the following section for now. Don't waste your time and build any expectations about being a better father if you're not willing to do what it takes. Recovery is tough. Recovery is for the courageous; it's not for cowards.

*Skip this section if you're **not** willing to do what it takes to be a better father.*

****

Step 1:

Get on your knees and acknowledge to God that your life is out of control. Get gut-level honest. Tell him about all of the things that you have done that are not in accordance with his will for you. That's right all the lust, the pornography, the teasing and flirting, any marriages that you may have destroyed (including your own), any people that you have harmed, the women you have objectified, the women in the chat rooms that you have led on, and the things that you have thought about doing (but didn't have the guts to carry out), being unable to be present for your children as you would like to have been, being unable (because of your addiction) to be the best example you could have been. Then ask for God's forgiveness. I know it sounds like a lot, but that's the cost of freedom. If you want to be free of your addiction, it will cost you--freedom aint free! But freedom through Christ is worth it!

Step 2:

If you have an addiction, get help. This one is a little harder because men have egos--huge egos. It seems that the more messed up we are the bigger our egos are. So, many men will have difficulty admitting that they have a problem and even more trouble admitting that they are an addict. So, how do you know if you are an addict? Actually, the answer to that question is not as important as you might think. If you can't stop, then you're an addict. You've already shared with God all of the things that you did that were not in accordance with his will. So, just stop. That's right. Never look at pornography again (not another pornographic website, video, or magazine), never flirt with a woman you aren't married to (no more flirtatious talk, no more chat rooms, no more sexting), never have sex with anyone other than your wife. If these behaviors are not obsessive, compulsive, addictive, you'll be able to stop. You don't need to get any additional help. You won't even have to ask God to take these desires away because they are within your control.

If you're still reading, then, yes, you're an addict (see Appendices for assessments). Get help. You need someone you can talk to who can assist you. You may want to talk to a therapist or counselor, an interventionist, a relationship specialist, a sex specialist, a sponsor, a person in the clergy, or seek out a recovery program. You need to find someone who you can talk about these issues with, and it needs to be someone who is healthy enough to not judge you, and someone who is skilled and knowledgeable enough to be able to assist you. You will need to tell them about your past. Yes, telling God is not sufficient. The person you select to assist you will be able to tell you how much they need to know and the limitations (for example, if a therapist or counselor learns that you have engaged in certain types of criminal activity, they are required to report it).

Step 3

Get help. You may want to contact a counselor or therapist. You may choose to seek help from a lay counselor affiliated with your religion or a civic organization. You may choose to get help from a support group. You might identify a sponsor to assist you. Many people in recovery benefit from a combination of the resources. These individuals will be an important part of your recovery.

Step 4

Carry out the plan for your recovery. Every day there will be things that you will need to do, or avoid, in order to stay on the path of recovery. You'll need to have one or more people that you can be accountable to. This person may be an accountability partner, a mentor, or a sponsor. This person will help you follow your plan for staying in recovery from your addiction while also trying to live in the real world as you go to work, school, and interact with other people who are important to you.

As children develop they look for models, other people around them who they can emulate and be like when they grow up. So, living a life of sexual integrity is important for you, but it's vital for your children because when they are very young they don't have to ability to distinguish between what they should do and what they shouldn't do. For young children, if Daddy is doing it, it must be the right thing to do. Are you presenting a godly example of fatherhood for your children?

If you're serious about being a better father, that's what you need to do. If you've lied to yourself and tried to convince yourself that making more money will make you a better father, you were wrong. If you told yourself that if you helped them with their homework more, that would make you a better father, you were wrong. If you told yourself that if you buy your children more presents and gifts that would make you a better father, you're wrong. None of those things is more important than addressing your addiction. If you are lusting after women through pornography, videos, chat rooms, and websites, then you're cheating your children of your time and attention. If you're flirting, either virtually, through text messages (sexting), the Web, or in person then you're having or trying to start an emotional affair and you're cheating your children of your time and attention. If you are having an affair, you're cheating your children of the opportunity of seeing their father as a man who can remain faithful to his wife. Your daughters need to know that men can be faithful to thei wives, so, they can have that as an expectation in their own marriages. Our sons need to see that their father can be faithful to his wife so that we can set a good example for them to follow. Like it or not it is very likely that your son will be a lot like you.

So, in order to be a better father, first, you need to deal with the issues that keep you from having the ability to be fully present in your relationship. Secondly, you need to deal with the issues that keep you from having the ability to have high levels of integrity in that relationship. Getting recovery from your pornography addiction, sex addiction, or love addiction will allow you to be fully present and give you the capability to be authentic with yourself and with your children.

****

*Continue here for those who were **not** willing to do what it takes to be a better father.*

v do I pursue my purpose, and experience a sense of fulfillment and achievement?

ᴣ into recovery and finding some relief from
many addicts become discouraged and

overwhelmed while trying to figure out how to stay sober and how to achieve their goals and dreams.

Porn and sex addicts are often people who are very, very driven. Because porn and sex addicts are so driven, you will see them excel in virtually every career area: doctors, lawyers, pastors, teachers, professors, accountants, etc. As the lust, porn, sex, and love addict is trying to climb the professional ladder, suddenly, because of the pain of his life, he realizes that he has an addiction. He's used to focusing on his career and excelling there. But now his world has come crashing down around him because of his addiction, because his wife found his porn, because he's been fired for looking at porn using his work computer, because his wife, co-workers, or his mistresses' husband discovered his affair. Because of circumstances, he's gotten into recovery. Of course, he thinks that after a few weeks, maybe a few months, he will have this addiction kicked and can go back to his normal life, minus the addiction.

After several months go by, he begins to realize that for the rest of his life he will have to work some kind of recovery program. He begins to realize that his life will never be the same. He thought that his life would continue to be the same, only without the addiction and it accompanying chaos. At about this time there is also great frustration because he wonders how he can achieve all of the great dreams that he has if he has to do all of this recovery work. How can he balance recovery with the rest of his life? How can he balance recovery along with being a husband, father, worker, business owner, or community volunteer? There aren't enough hours in the day to do it all. The key is that he doesn't balance it. His recovery has to come first.

Unhealthy Things Men Do - Anything you put before your recovery, you'll lose.

If you don't do your recovery work because you are spending every possible waking moment with your wife, i.e. if you put your wife before your recovery, you'll lose her. If you're a sex addict and you don't work your program, you'll end up acting out again and you'll lose your wife, because if you continue to act out she'll leave. You 've to work your program because you're an addict. By 'tion, you are unable to stop on your own. Anything before your recovery program, you'll lose. You e your recovery program--you prioritize it!

There are many approaches to helping people overcome addiction to pornography, lust, and sex addiction. I'll share the approach that I use.

Chapter 5

My Approach to Sponsorship

I have been very fortunate to have found recovery. I am so thankful that God created recovery programs for lust, pornography, sex, and love addiction. My road to sexual purity and sexual integrity has involved recovery from all four of these. I have been blessed by great sponsorship. I have a primary sponsor and backup sponsor. At the time of this writing, I have several people that I can contact as part of my recovery.

In my personal recovery program, sponsorship is something that I have the pleasure of doing to assist others on a voluntary basis. In addition, there are times that I have been blessed to be able to conduct workshops for organizations and serve as a recovery-mentor/consultant for other individuals and couples who would like assistance regarding understanding and overcoming lust,
ʳnography, sex, and love addiction.

ʾpproach to sponsorship (and recovery
ʹconsulting) is pretty hands-on. Here are some
ʰich guide my process of sponsoring others:

- For pornography and sex addiction, I believe the driving force is lust. Hence, the pursuit of pornography and sex is just a manifestation of lust and the thinking that leads to lust.

- Merely stopping the behaviors is not sufficient. The addict's thinking must eventually change. The thinking drives the behavior.

- Sexual purity, sexual integrity, and sexual sobriety are terms that I use interchangeably.

- For those individuals and couples that I work with, sexual purity, sexual integrity, sexual sobriety are defined by the following characteristics:

  (1) They do not use pornography.

  (2) They only have sex with their spouse.

  (3) Sex must be consensual.

  (4) They don't engage in online/virtual sexual relationships.

  (5) No self-masturbation.

- They have to be willing to reach out for help and make contact once a day for the first 90 days to be accountable for their behavior and recovery.

- Read recovery literature daily.

- Pray daily.

- Meditate.

- Plan.
- Actively work a recovery program and be willing to do so indefinitely.
- (Note: in working with individuals and couples in the role of recovery-mentor, relationship coach, our plan includes a limited time frame, it's not indefinite).

Chapter 6

What Does Healthy Love Look Like?

Many addicts addicted to lust, pornography, sex, or love end up getting help because of the impact that their addiction has had on one or more important relationships. Of course, many of us have told those close to us that we love them, even though, often, our behavior did not match our words. The sad truth is that many of us don't know what love is. Love is not a feeling. Love is expressed through acts of service and through sacrifice.

In his book, *The Road Less Traveled*, M. Scott Peck describes love as the process of taking the actions that enhance your spiritual development and the spiritual development of the person you say you love. In other words, loving yourself involves taking the actions that help you enhance your relationship with God and enhance your overall emotional well-being. Loving someone else involves taking actions that help that person enhance their relationship with God and enhance your overall emotional well-being. Love involves the ability and willingness to serve another person. Before recovery, many of my actions were not loving. Many of the things I did in hopes of getting sex from the woman I was dating at the time were manipulative, not loving.

Love also involves the ability and willingness to sacrifice for another person. In the Bible, God describes the most important measure of true love; it's the ability to sacrifice for another person. Love suffers long and is kind; love does not envy; love does not parade itself, is not puffed up (I Corinthians 13:4; New King James Version). As the Bible says, love suffers long. From one of the most often recited passages of scripture: "For God so loved the world that He gave His only begotten Son, that whoever believes in Him should not perish but have everlasting life" (John 3:16; New King James Version). Because God loved us he gave, he sacrificed his son. True love is demonstrated through serving others and through the ability and willingness to sacrifice for others.

Part II

An Original Recipe:

Key Aspects of my Approach to Sponsorship

Chapter 7

Tell Yourself the Truth

As an addict, I was used to lying to myself, convincing myself that I really didn't have a problem, and that all men need and think about sex much of the time, that being obsessive and compulsive about sex and pornography was normal in spite of the fact that it was wreaking havoc in my relationship. Not to mention that in my faith, like most major religions, I was supposed to be waiting until marriage to have sex.

Telling the truth is vital. You can't expect to remain sober from sexual acting out and lust if you are unable to be honest. So, how do you learn to be honest? If you have a good sponsor, he'll be able to tell pretty quickly if you're being honest. After working with several addicts, the patterns are pretty easy to spot and the lies can be detected. Also, it's impossible to stay sober if you're lying about your acting out. Also, if you lie about your acting out, you're hurting yourself. You won't stay sober and the consequences of acting out are substantial, up to and including death. Unfortunately, suicide is a reality for addicts when the pain becomes too great.

If you have a good sponsor and you actually use your sponsor, he'll be able to detect if you're lying and call you on your dishonesty. I believe in rigorous honesty. I believe in cutting to the chase because that's where we need to get in order to have recovery and the kind of life that God wants for his children.

Chapter 8

Journal

Sex addicts in general have difficulty making wise decisions, especially in areas in which the addiction may be impacted. Often as addicts, even in recovery, especially during the first couple of years of recovery, we have difficulty making decisions. Also, addicts are often unaware and not present, and fly or live on automatic pilot. This is one of the reasons why sponsorship is so important. As they often say in sex recovery programs, your best thinking led you to act sexually in ways that were harmful to you and others.

One of the best ways to examine what you do is to keep a journal. Often as an addict, before recovery, you probably went through your day and could not remember the details of what happened. Sure, you might remember the big things like going to work or dropping your child off at school. But, do you remember what your wife was upset about this morning? Do you remember why you were tempted to look at porn this morning? Do you remember why you made the flirtatious comment to your co-worker? Do you remember the brief fantasy that you had as you drove by the strip club to get to work?

Journaling, the process of writing down what happens during the day, is vital for recovering sex addicts. If you're serious about having an enhanced relationship with God, a stronger recovery, and being fully present in your own life, recovery journaling is a must. Some people choose to journal by using a pen or pencil and a notebook or a bound book with lined or unlined pages. Some recovering sex addicts choose to type out their journal on a computer. No matter what form it's in, you should keep it secure so that your children or visitors to your home don't accidentally find and read it. If it's on a computer, you should keep it secure with a password or, even better, with security software so you wife or children don't accidentally open it.

You need to keep a journal for all of the following reasons:

- It will help you to think about what happened during the day; this helps you to get out of the living-by-autopilot mode. If you journal at night you can reflect on the day. If you journal in the morning you can reflect on the previous day.
- It helps you to look at your actions during the day.
- It helps you to examine your thoughts that occurred during the day. It's the thinking that leads to the acting out behaviors, so examining your thinking is vital.

- As you implement various recovery tools, you can use your journaling to help determine which tools work and how well. For example, if you start praying every morning asking God to keep you sober for the day, in your journal at the end of the day, you can see if the prayer had an impact on your day. Maybe it helped for the first part of the day and you could tell that you were more cautious and purposely avoided certain triggers. Through your journaling you may have discovered that in addition to praying in the morning when you first get up, you may also need to pray again at lunch time asking God to keep you sober for the remainder of the day.

- You can use journaling to examine what's really going on when you feel emotionally disturbed. This is a huge deal. It took me years to get to the point where I could actually recognize and admit that I was emotionally disturbed. So, what do I mean when I talk about being emotionally disturbed? It's the gut-level feeling that you need to take action now! But, you sometimes don't really know why. It's when you feel like you want to leave your body and go somewhere else or do something else. It's the feeling of wanting to run away, but you don't know where to go. You just know that you have to get away from where you are right now. When you're emotionally disturbed, there is usually something else going on underneath.

- For the last 13 years, I have been assisting people in the process of dealing with their addiction of lust, sex, and love, and there is usually something else underneath when they are emotionally disturbed. The issues that are causing someone to be emotionally disturbed can often be summarized by the following acrostic: HALTS. HALTS stands for Hungry, Angry, Lonely, Tired, Stressed. If you are in a high HALTS state, very hungry, angry, lonely, tired, or stressed, you will probably feel emotionally disturbed. Since addictive behavior is often used as a means to escape from uncomfortable emotions, this can trigger lust, which often leads to the need to escape through viewing pornography, sex, etc.

- You can also use journaling to enhance your relationship with God. I used this technique during a time in my recovery when I was staying sober, but didn't have any joy. And, quite frankly, I wanted to get past the feelings of self-pity and resentment about having to be in recovery. As if that were not enough, my relationship with God was not strong like I wanted it to be. So, I used a slightly different technique to my journaling. I began tracking all of the blessings that God was bestowing upon me. Some of the blessings were small, like getting a great parking spot at a store, at work, or at school. Some of the blessings were big, like staying in recovery and having great sponsors and a great recovery team to help me (sponsors, coaches, accountability partners, etc.). I tracked all of them and over time, not overnight, my relationship with God grew. I was able to see that although things didn't always turn out the way that I wanted them to, I have been blessed abundantly. Also, one of the other benefits is that the more you start looking for God's blessings, the easier it is to recognize them; and you'll notice that you'll see them much more often. This is the great upward spiral of seeing Gods' blessings. I call it God's spiral of joy. I've been using a journal for a while. I now have over 27,000 blessings that I've recorded.

Chapter 9

Pray and Meditate

Prayer is a powerful tool used by millions of people around the globe. There are dozens of books that have been written to teach people more about prayer. Prayer is just talking to God. For those of us in recovery, prayer must be a priority. If you could solve you own problems related to your sex addiction, you would have done so a long time ago. You can't solve your problem by yourself. But, with God's help you can. Talk to Him! God loves and wants you to have a very full life. But, we are not designed to have a life without being plugged in to the source of our lives--God. Remember, anything you put before your recovery you will lose. Your recovery is integral to your relationship with God.

Prayer involves talking to God. So, what kinds of things should you talk to God about: well, if you're serious about your recovery, you'll talk to God about everything that's important to you: your fears, problems, worries, and joys. You may talk to Him just to thank him for another hour or another day of sobriety. You may want to thank him for your recovery team, your job, your church, and the opportunities that he has given you to help others. At a minimum, you should pray in the morning, asking God to keep you sober and lust-free for today, and at night, thanking Him for the day and asking him to keep you sober and free from lust throughout the night, and asking him to bless your recovery support team. Of course, you will probably want to include other things in your prayer, but these are the bare minimums in relation to your recovery.

Over time as you talk to God on a regular basis, you may find yourself talking to him more throughout the day, not just in the morning and at night. Just like in your other relationships, the level of closeness is highly dependent upon the frequency and depth of communication. If you don't talk frequently, you won't have much of a relationship. But, also, if you don't have any in depth conversations, if you only talk about superficial things like the weather or your sports teams, you won't have much depth in the relationship. The goal is to communicate with God so that you have great frequency and great depth. We discussed the first half of the communication process with God, prayer--talking to God. But that's only half of your communication with God.

Prayer and meditation go together. Prayer is talking to God, telling him about your problems, fears, etc. Meditation is listening to God for the answers, for His wisdom, for direction for your life. Talking to God is important. You have to be able to vent and share your thoughts and feelings in any relationship in order for there to be a relationship. Have you ever been in a relationship where the other person always wanted to talk about their problems, their issues, and what was important to them, but they never wanted to listen? After several instances, did you feel like a dumping ground? Yes, that's the kind of person who wants to complain, but they are not willing to hear what you have to say because they don't want to change. They didn't ask for your feedback because they don't want it.

Meditation is the process in which you listen for God's direction and guidance. There are various methods for meditation, but the most important aspects of meditation are the following:

- Get into a quiet position, usually sitting down.
- Quiet your mind. This can be done by quietly repeating a phrase in your head to keep you focused and calm. When other thoughts come to mind, they will leave if you continue to repeat the phrase. You can also focus on your breathing to quiet your mind.
- Comfortable clothing.
- Close your eyes.

- Turn off all electronic equipment: phone, television, radio, etc.

Warning!: you'll have to do this several times before you get comfortable with the concept of accomplishing something by doing nothing. It's very counter-intuitive. Don't give up. Give God the opportunity to talk to you. Even if you can only do this for 1 minute when you first start, don't give up. One minute is better than no minutes. Ideally, try to build up to 15 or 30 minute time frame. If you can do this daily, you'll see health benefits of being more relaxed, and hearing from God. If that's too much to start with then start just meditating on the weekends.

Prayer and meditation . . . talking to God and listening to God. I think of prayer as talking to God with the purpose of talking about your thoughts, fears, anger, resentment, etc. and giving thanks. On the other hand meditation is the process of quieting down and listening for God's responses to those concerns. Also during meditation God may provide direction about some personal action that you should take or He may direct you to assist others in some way. Using prayer and meditation together, is one of the keys to authentic, two-way communication with God. This is vital for your recovery.

Chapter 10

Exercise

For sex addicts, the addiction is not just in our minds, through lusting and the pursuit of acting out, it's also in our blood stream. When a sex addict is pursuing sex and scores a hit, in terms of his brain chemistry, it is the equivalent of getting a hit of cocaine. As suggested by sex research, sex addicts often have an altered neuro-chemistry, the chemicals in the sex addict's brain is similar to those who are addicted to cocaine (Note 1).

So, if you aren't acting out any more to get the hit, what do you do? Exercise. The endorphins you receive from exercise will help you in several ways. You will tend to have more energy throughout the day due to exercise. This is important because when you stop acting out you may have a noticeable lack of energy. Exercising can also help to regulate your sleep. Keep in mind that for sex addicts often their acting out takes place late at night or early in the morning when they're less likely to be interrupted. Also, in the early stages of recovery when you feel like you just have to act out or you'll die, running three miles or playing a game of racquetball can really take the edge off.

Chapter 11

Read

Yes, read.   Sex addicts do spend time reading, but unfortunately the things that bring the most enjoyment, and pain, are the same things which feed the addiction.   It is not uncommon for a sex addict (who's avenue of choice is porn, texting, or chat rooms) to spend hundreds of hours over the course of a year reading online porn, texting, or chatting online.   Yes, hundreds of hours.   Some addicts spend over 100 hours looking at online porn in a month.

In recovery, you have to use your reading ability to put things into your mind that draw you closer to God and further away from your addiction.   Sex addicts who are in active addiction want to have lust and sex in their minds so they fill their minds with pornography and vehicles of lust. Sex addicts in recovery must fill their minds with recovery, with seeing other men and woman as children of God, not sex and lust objects.   In recovery, you have to fill your mind with information and knowledge to fill the hole in your soul that the lust was trying to fill.

So, what should you read? Here is the short list:

- Recovery literature about sex addiction that provides solutions about dealing with sex addiction. I read a page of sexual integrity or sex addiction recovery literature every day.

- The real focus is on sexual integrity and striving to live free of lust because lust drives the sexual thinking and behavior. In the recovery process, there is a subtle difference between sexual addiction and sexual integrity. Sexual addiction asks the question: How badly do I have to destroy my life before I get help? Whereas sexual integrity asks these two questions: (1) Am I living a life of sexual integrity? (2) If not, I am going to take action now to get on track before things get worse. The sexual addiction perspective takes a reactive approach; this usually occurs when a person has hit rock bottom. Rock bottom for some people is lower than it is for others. The sexual integrity perspective takes a proactive approach. It involves taking action to address the issues of sexual thinking and behavior so you don't have to hit rock bottom and lose everything. Also, if you have other addictions or obsessive /compulsive issues, read recovery literature about that addiction that focuses on solutions and what you can do to get better (Note: many sex addicts have multiple addictions. It's very common to have a sex addiction and any one of the following: drug addiction, alcohol addiction, gambling addiction, eating disorder, codependence, etc.). I read a page from an adult children of alcoholics, love addiction, or codependence book every day.

- If you're married, engaged, or dating someone, you need to read a book about healthy relationships because if you're an addict you don't know how to have a healthy relationship, but it's not too late to learn. Every day I read a page from marriage literature to learn more about healthy marriages.

- If you're a parent, read about being a better parent. I read a weekly online parenting publication.

- If you have a faith tradition, you should read about it. I read a chapter of my Bible daily. Also, you may be able to find a recovery version of the book. I have an NIV (New International Version) Recovery Devotional Bible. It's a regular NIV Bible and in the margins they show how various recovery steps and concepts are correlated to various scriptures in the Bible. This is a great way to help those in recovery understand how the truths within the Bible can be directly applied to porn, sex, lust, and love addiction.

- A book about a goal that you want to achieve: going back to college, starting your own business, being more effective at work, being a better parent, being a better spouse, or for those who aren't married, preparing to be a great spouse.

- An inspirational book about overcoming obstacles or a book about being effective as a person, worker, etc: *The Power of Positive Thinking* by Dr. Norman Vincent Peale, *Man's Search for Meaning* by Viktor Frankel, *The 7 Habits of Highly Effective People* and *First Things First* both by Dr. Stephen Covey, etc. and biographies of great leaders.

I read from a total of 15 books in the morning. It may sound a little overwhelming, but I only read a page from each book and I read a chapter from my Bible (which is sometimes more than one page).

Chapter 12

Plan

When I work as part of a recovery support team, one of the key things that I ask the recovering addict is: "What is your plan for the rest of the day?" or "What is your plan for tomorrow?" An addict without a plan is a disaster looking for a place to happen.

If you're serious about your recovery, you must have a plan for maintaining your recovery on a daily basis. Rather than thinking about what you need to do to stay sober for the rest of your life, or what you need to fix so you can act out without suffering consequences, the more important question is: What is your plan for the rest of the day? Yes, you have to ensure that you incorporate your recovery into your day. Actually, you need to put key recovery components into place for the day and then put in the other stuff, like work, family time, eating, and sleeping. Yes, it may sound strange to put your recovery first, but if you don't you'll end up losing everything else anyway.

I've had the joy and privilege of helping people build solid marriages and recover from sex and lust addiction for over a decade. I can assure you that if you don't put your recovery and your relationship with God first, you'll lose everything else. Remember: your recovery program is really your plan to build a strong relationship with God. Even if you're fortunate enough to not lose everything, you will not be able to have the happy, fulfilled life that God desires for you. Recovery must come first.

Two important planning questions are:
(1) What is your plan for the rest of the day?
(2) What is your plan for tomorrow?

Here is a good sample plan if you're a *morning* person:

- Pray: awaken early, drop down on your knees and pray. In the prayer, be sure to ask God to keep you sober and lust-free today. Also, include thanks within your prayer for your current sobriety and recovery, and other blessings.
- Meditate (even if it's only one minute)
- Exercise
- Read
- Journal
- Prepare for the day: Examine your plan for the day [As you look at your plan for the day, briefly focus on the key activities today: be mindful of any activities, tasks, or meetings that may be triggering, things that may put

you in a high HALTS state (Hungry, Angry/Afraid, Lonely, Tired, Stressed)].

If you identify things that may put you in a high HALTS state, prepare in advance for the challenge. Here is a short list of some things you can do: keep the phone number of some of your recovery support team members available, also keep note of what times they are likely to be available; keep key Bible verses handy. If you will be attending a meeting or other necessary function in which a potential lust object (someone who triggers lust for you or someone you're attracted to) will be present, pray for the person in advance and be prepared to continue to pray for them when you get there. When challenged, some recovering addicts have trouble remembering what to pray. The Lust Brain Freeze occurs. So another recommendation is to put together a Lust-Free prayer/Sexual Purity Prayer/Sexual Integrity Prayer (See below for components). Create a prayer and memorize it (see the format below).

If you happen to be in a meeting and you aren't able to concentrate enough to pray, here is another technique that is very effective. Journal and write about your frustration. Don't be too explicit about the issue because someone may ask to look at your notes. But, typically people will just assume that you're taking notes about what's happening at the meeting. . Very, very rarely will anyone even think twice about what you're writing. Also, it's better for you to get the thoughts and issues out of your head than to have them impact your interaction with your colleagues. Remember, people have very short memories when you do something right, but they have very long memories when you do something wrong.

- Work and/or school
- Family Time
- Wind Down (pray, reflect on the day, you may even want to do some additional journaling about things that occurred during the day). This is a great way to release the events of the day and prepare for a restful night's sleep.

- Lust-Free /Sexual Purity /Sexual Integrity Prayer components (1) acknowledge that sexual purity is a challenge for you and you need God's help, (2) acknowledge that you don't want to think thoughts or take actions that are impure, (3) ask God to keep your thoughts, actions, and motives pure, (4) thank God for the opportunity to grow closer to Him during this challenge and temptation.
- Review Key Bible verses (see Appendix A). You may also want to have these available so you can refer to them when you need them.

Here is a good sample plan if you're an *evening* person

- MORNING: Pray: awaken early, drop down on your knees and pray. Yes, even evening people have to pray first thing in the morning. In the prayer be sure to ask God to keep you sober and lust-free today. Also, include thanks within your prayer for your current sobriety and recovery, and other blessings.
- MORNING: Meditate (even if it's only one minute)
- EVENING: Exercise
- EVENING: Read
- EVENING: Journal

- EVENING: Examine your plan for tomorrow and be mindful of any activities, tasks, or meetings that may put you in a high HALTS state (Hungry, Angry/Afraid, Lonely, Tired, Stressed). If you identify things that may put you in a high HALTS state, prepare in advance for the challenge by doing one or more of the following: keeping the phone number of some of your recovery support team members available, also keep note of what times they are likely to be available; keeping Bible verses available to meditate on. If you will be attending a meeting or another necessary function in which a potential lust object will be present, pray for the person in advance and be prepared to continue to pray for them when you get there. When in challenging situations, some recovering addicts have trouble remembering what to pray, so another recommendation is to put together a Lust-Free or Sexual Purity Prayer (see below). If you happen to be in a meeting and you aren't able to concentrate enough to pray, here is another technique that is very effective. Journal and write about your frustration. Don't be too explicit about the issue because someone may ask to look at your notes. But, typically people will just assume that you're taking notes on the meeting. Very,

very rarely will anyone even think twice about what you're writing. Also, it's better for you to get the thoughts and issues out of your head than to have it impact your interaction with your colleagues. Remember, if you do something right you will hear a few positive comments about it, but if you do something wrong you may never hear the end of it. Work and/or school

- Family Time
- EVENING: Wind Down (pray, reflect on the day, you may even want to do some additional journaling about things that occurred during the day). As you pray remember to release your day and your feelings about the day to the Lord, so he can grant you rest.
- Sexual Purity Prayer components: (1) acknowledge that sexual purity is a challenge for you and you can't handle it without God's help, (2) acknowledge that you don't want to think thoughts or take actions that are impure, (3) cast your temptations to lust and act out onto God and ask him to take them from you, (4) ask God to keep your thoughts and actions sexually pure, (5) thank God for the opportunity to grow closer to Him during this challenge and temptation.
- Review Key Bible verses (see Appendix A)

Check-in Regularly/ Accountability

The regular checking in is very important. Addicts are not used to being accountable. But, in order to address the issues of addiction, accountability has to be one of the cornerstones of your recovery plan. The measure of your ability to take suggestions and follow-through will be the measure of your willingness to deal with your addiction and restore and enhance your life and key relationships.

Often the people who seek help from their sex addiction are married or engaged and the pressure from the spouse or spouse-to-be drives them to seek some help. Remember that there is help and hope if you're willing to ask for it and follow prudent guidance from your recovery support team. That team may consist of only one person or multiple people.

If you want to add me to your recovery support team or would like for me to speak to your group or organization about the importance of healthy marriages and integrity in marriage, feel free to contact me.

Notes:

Chapter 10

Stanley Sunderwirth, Harvey Milkman, and Nancy Jenks, "Neurochemistry and Sexual Addiction," Sexual Addiction and Compulsiviy 3, No. 1 (1996)

APPENDICES

Appendix A

Key Bible Verses

¹³I can do all things through Christ which strengtheneth me.

Philippians 4:13 (King James Version)

1 Corinthians 10:13

There hath **no temptation taken** you but such as is common to man: but God is faithful, who will **not** suffer you to be tempted above that ye are able; but will with the **temptation** also make a way to escape, that ye may be able to bear it.

Proverbs 6:32

But whoso committeth **adultery** with a woman lacketh understanding: he that doeth it destroyeth his own soul.

Matthew 5:28

But I say unto you, That whosoever looketh on a woman to lust after her hath committed **adultery** with her already in his heart.

Genesis 2:24

Therefore shall a man leave his father and his mother, and shall cleave unto his **wife**: and they shall be one flesh.

Proverbs 5:18

Let thy fountain be blessed: and rejoice with the **wife** of thy youth.

Proverbs 6:29

So he that goeth in to his **neighbour's wife**; whosoever toucheth her shall not be innocent.

Proverbs 18:22

Whoso findeth a **wife** findeth a good thing, and obtaineth favour of the LORD.

Matthew 19:5

And said, For this cause shall a man leave father and mother, and shall cleave to his wife: and they twain shall be **one flesh**?

1 Corinthians 7:2

Nevertheless, to **avoid fornication**, let every man have his own **wife**, and let every woman have her own husband.

Ephesians 5:28

So ought men to love their wives as their own bodies. He that **loveth his wife** loveth himself.

Appendix B

Love Addiction Assessment

Love Addiction involves being dependent on and enmeshed with another person. The sense of dependency involves the love addict feeling as though they can't make it without the other person and placing too much value upon another person. Because the life of the love addict is so entangled with the life of the partner, the love addict doesn't have their own sense of identity. In addition, love addicts are often drawn to partners who are not emotionally available and who are unable to meet their unrealistic expectations of continuous love, encouragement, and support.

Are you a love addict?

Were you quickly attracted to someone who you later learned was unable or unwilling to make time for you (someone who was emotionally unavailable)?
Yes_____ No_____

Has the other person described you as being needy?
Yes_____ No_____

Has the other person stated on multiple occasions (or shown through their actions) that they need their space or that they need to be away from you for a while?
Yes_____ No_____

Has the other person found ways to distance themselves from you as a result of your neediness (spending extra time at work, getting involved with other people or organizations)?
Yes_____ No_____

Has the other person stated that you were taking too much of their time, hovering over them, smothering them, etc.?
Yes_____ No_____

Do you feel that having the right relationship will make you feel complete? Yes_____ No_____

Do you feel a tremendous, almost overwhelming, sense of sadness at the thought of the relationship ending even though you are very unhappy in the relationship?
Yes_____ No_____

Have you had a cycle of being attracted to people who were emotionally unavailable? Yes_____ No_____

The more questions you answer "yes" the more love addict characteristics you have.

Reference: Pia Melody, Andrea Wells Miller, J. Keith Miller, Facing Love Addiction (New York, HarperCollins, 1992).

Appendix C

Sex Addiction Assessment

Sex addiction involves obsessive and compulsive sexual behavior that usually has negative consequences. And, in spite of negative consequences the addict continues to engage in the destructive sexual behavior. These consequences may involve personal guilt, damaged personal relationships, being emotionally unavailable, job loss, loss of a romantic relationship or marriage, or in extreme cases even incarceration or death.

Is your sexual thinking and behavior obsessive and compulsive? Are you a sex addict?

Do you obsessively or compulsively view pornography (via magazines, DVDs, Internet, etc.)? Yes_____ No_____

Do you regularly view pornography (via magazines, DVDs, Internet, etc.) daily, weekly? Yes_____ No_____

Have you paid for sex? Yes_____ No_____

Have you had guilt about your sexual behavior?
Yes_____ No_____

Have you lied about your sexual behavior?
Yes_____ No_____

While in a committed relationship (marriage, engagement, etc.), have you had sex with someone else?
Yes_____ No_____

Do you fantasize about other sexual partners during sex?
Yes_____ No_____

Have you used company equipment (computers etc.) to view pornographic material? Yes_____ No_____

Have you lost a job because of your sexual behavior?
Yes_____ No_____

Have you had engaged in emotional affairs (flirting and trying to connect emotionally for sex via face-to-face, in chat rooms, Internet, social media, etc.)?
Yes_____ No_____

Have you had one or more sexual affairs?
Yes_____ No_____

Have you had a sexually transmitted disease?
Yes_____ No_____

Have you lost a marriage (or primary romantic relationship for those who aren't married) because of your sexual behavior? Yes_____ No_____

Have you engaged in sexual behavior that could have led to criminal punishment? Yes_____ No_____

The more questions you answer "yes" the more sex addiction characteristics you have.

Appendix D

Resources

Organizations

National Association for Christian Recovery
Snail mail: NACR, P.O. Box 3771, Richmond, VA 23235
Voice: 562-252-3737 Extension 1
Fax: 888-504-0989
http://www.nacronline.com

American Association for Christian Counselors
PO Box 739
Forest, VA 24551
1.800.526.8673
http://www.aacc.net

Sex Addiction Recovery Groups

Sexaholics Anonymous
P.O. Box 3565
Brentwood, TN 37024
Phone: (615) 370-6062
Toll-free: (866) 424-8777
www.sa.org

Sexual Compulsives Anonymous
SCA P.O. Box 1585
Old Chelsea Station
New York, NY 10011
Phone: (800) 977-HEAL
http://www.sca-recovery.org/

Sex Addicts Anonymous
ISO of SAA
PO Box 70949
Houston, TX 77270 USA
Email: info@saa-recovery.org
Phone: (800) 477-8191
http://www.sexaa.org/

Sex and Love Addicts Anonymous
1550 NE Loop 410, Ste 118
San Antonio, TX 78209
Email: info@slaafws.org
Phone: (210) 828-7900
Fax: (001) 210-828-7922
http://www.slaafws.org/

Love Addiction and Codependent Recovery Groups

S-Anon
P.O. Box 111242
Nashville, TN 37222-1242
E-mail: sanon@sanon.org
Phone: (800) 210-8141 or (615) 833-3152
http://www.sanon.org/

Al-Anon
Al-Anon Family Group Headquarers, Inc.
1600 Corporate Landing Parkway
Virginia Beach, VA 23454-5617
(888)425-2666
http://www.al-anon.alateen.org/english.html

International Service Organization of COSA (or ISO of
COSA)
PO Box 79908
Houston TX 77279-9908 U.S.A.
Phone: (866) 899-COSA   (866) 899-COSA (2672)
E-Mail: info@cosa-recovery.org
http://www.cosa-recovery.org/

Codependents Anonymous
CoDA, Fellowship Services Office
PO Box 33577
Phoenix, AZ 85067-3577
(888) 444-2359
http://www.coda.org/

About the Author

Dr. Simon Whittaker is a recovery mentor, relationship expert, and former host of the Radio Talk Show, Relationship Fridays. He provides relationship coaching to couples and serves as a recovery mentor to countless numbers of men, assisting them in overcoming lust, porn, sex, and love addiction. He also develops personal development programs used in his coaching relationships to help people meet their personal and professional objectives. He and his wife, Dr. Tyra Whittaker, also conduct couples workshops and assist engaged couples through the pre-marital counseling ministry at their local church.

If you would like to add Dr. Whittaker to your recovery support team or would like for him to speak to your group or organization about the healthy marriages, sex addiction, or love addiction, he can be contacted at: info@whittakerinstitute.com, simonwhitt@gmail.com, or http://whittakerinstitute.com.

CPSIA information can be obtained at www.ICGtesting.com
Printed in the USA
BVOW06s0606030915

416338BV00007B/44/P